"At Their Mercy"

"At Their Mercy"

Junior Bodine

authorHOUSE®

AuthorHouse™ LLC
1663 Liberty Drive
Bloomington, IN 47403
www.authorhouse.com
Phone: 1-800-839-8640

© 2014 Junior Bodine. All rights reserved.

No part of this book may be reproduced, stored in
a retrieval system, or transmitted by any means
without the written permission of the author.

Published by AuthorHouse 04/10/2014

ISBN: 978-1-4969-0170-5 (sc)
ISBN: 978-1-4969-0171-2 (e)

Any people depicted in stock imagery provided by Thinkstock are models,
and such images are being used for illustrative purposes only.
Certain stock imagery © Thinkstock.

This book is printed on acid-free paper.

Because of the dynamic nature of the Internet, any web addresses or
links contained in this book may have changed since publication and
may no longer be valid. The views expressed in this work are solely those
of the author and do not necessarily reflect the views of the publisher,
and the publisher hereby disclaims any responsibility for them.

I dedicate this book to my wife
Margaret Scoggin
For without her there would be no book.

Contents

Introduction ix

Chapter 1	Bobbie Death 1
Chapter 2	The Truth About Malpractice 9
Chapter 3	Preventable Infection Fatalities 23
Chapter 4	Lawyers 28
Chapter 5	Doctors 36
Chapter 6	Nursing 40
Chapter 7	Numbers 42
Chapter 8	Conclusion—Final II—This is Master Copy 52

INTRODUCTION

Each year hundreds of thousands of patient are killed by preventable medical mistakes.

("Unaccountable" book by Marty Makary, MD)

This book is the authentic first hand story of one of these deaths; my wife's life and the accompanying malpractice lawsuit.

I was encouraged to file a lawsuit at the suggestion of a lawyer and a nurse. I love justice and have since I was a young boy. That is the reason I successfully pursued a Malpractice Law Suit.

I have always read; it moves me in a way that nothing else does. I read books by prominent lawyers of the past. I read Louis Nizer "My life in Court". Louis Nizer quote: "Still, I know of no higher fortitude than stubbornness in the face of overwhelming odds". I read the painfully honest autobiography of Gerry Spence "The Making of a Country Lawyer". I wrote Gerry Spence. In his answer to my letter he said "It is hard, very hard to get justice. Don't give Up!

This is the epic story of the struggle against justice and inhumanity.

Chapter 1

BOBBIE DEATH

Bobbie Jo Scoggin, my wife of 50 year, died suddenly and unexpectedly on July 19, 2004. Her death certificate, as certified by her physician, list "septic meningitis" as the immediate cause of her death and her manner of death as "Natural Death". I understand there was an addenda to her death certificate saying the medicine methotrexate masked her symptoms? She was taking methotrexate for her arthritis.

The term "Natural Death", as used, is an intriguing, puzzling term. It does not exist in medical terminology. It has been stricken from medical terminology. Texas Tech Medical School Library does not even list it even one time in the entire library. Amazingly doctors cannot certify any manner of death except "Natural Death"? (A non existent term). It is their default definition!

But if a patient dies within 24 hours of admission, a doctors cannot certify a death. He must call a medical examiner. The Handbook on Death Registration, on Page

6, says if the manner of death is other than "Natural Death" call the medical examiner.

It is understandable that the term "natural death" is no longer in use in modern day medicine. It is because, as a practical matter, the patient can be kept alive indefinitely blurring the meaning . . .

Bobbie's story begin two weeks earlier on July 2, 2004 when she had a surgery on her lower back to relieve the intense pain caused by her sciatic nerve—a simple micro decompression—the simplest operation that an orthopedic surgeon performs. She was told she would be walking the next day and she was. She had elected to have this operation to eliminate the pain in her lower back so she could get on with her life. For the two days before July 17th Bobbie was feeling good enough to keep Allie, our granddaughter.

The doctor stated her operation was a success. In fact, the physician was very proud that the incision he made was less than an inch long and he had only spilled a thimble of blood. Naturally I was elated; because sitting there in the waiting room, I had an unreasoned fear out of all proportion to reality that she might become paralyzed? How could we go from a perfect surgery to a catastrophic painful death? A fatal hospital acquired Infection named "spinal meningitis".

Her recovery seemed almost normal and uneventful until the evening of Friday July 16, 2004 (some 2 weeks after her sciatic nerve operation) when she complained about

"At Their Mercy"

being nauseated and started throwing up. She should have seen a doctor at this time.

I called the physician office and spoke with his physician assistant. Evidently he was asleep. He was late to answer the phone and sounded sleepily which deeply unnerved me but he perked up toward the end of the conversation and said "it did not warrant going to the emergency room". This was my first big mistake: I hung my hat on his word and did not immediately take Bobbie to the hospital. I trusted him! This was the PA's mistake also. He was not really concerned.

The next morning, July 17, 2004, Bobbie was sick and throwing up so I called 911. The ambulance took her to the Emergency Room at Covenant Medical Center where she and I sat all day with me in one of the little emergency rooms. This was the hospital big fatal mistake: delayed diagnosis. She should have been seen asap. Every one at this point is to blame.

There were two things that unnerved me. One was the physician Assistant was there at the emergency room but did not come in and examine Bobbie? When I asked the nurse about a doctor seeing Bobbie she said he was signed in? Another was Bobbie was asked to fill out the same paperwork twice? Did the right hand did not know what the left hand was doing? (I took it for granted, without giving it a second thought, that the hospital had her complete records—her medical history—showing she was elderly and had a week immune system and a list of the medications she was taking including methotrexate.)

Junior Bodine

After sitting in the little emergency examination room all day Bobbie was taken to a hospital room in mid afternoon. Once in room #598, Bobbie's throwing up worsen. She was throwing up every 4 minutes (I counted them) despite morphine injection. She became deathly ill. She complained of her lower back hurting. She begged for help "Somebody Help Me". I complained to the two room nurses who were in and out attending to other rooms. Finally one said "we are trying to call the doctor". (This was a weekend and I understand Dr D'Alise was out of town and whoever was filling in for him had to be called 5 times before he was reached.) Nurses should have called another doctors at this point.

How do I get her attended to? It was madding, frustrating and bewildering! Bobbie complained about the pain in her head and upper back which were not diminishing. I could not get anyone's attention for my efforts. The nurses did not answer my questions as they whisked in and out. When I went to the nurses' station I was ignored! At this point I should have asserted myself and demanded help.

The next time I complained to the first nurses who did not answer me and to the second nurse who over talked me! So I went to the nurses' station. I stepped squarely up to the counter, got the attention of the young nurse and told her I was "upset". She said she would check? AT this point I should have called the hospital supervisor or administrator.

The very next time the first nurse returned to the room she told me she had talked to the doctor and he told her to continue what they were doing (giving her morphine),

"At Their Mercy"

The atmosphere was one of frustration and hostility. At this point I should have blown my top.

The hospital's job was to attend to her. I had no other choice; but I had trepidations!

So, completely exhausted. I went home to get some sleep.

Bobbie called me after I got in bed and I will never forget how she closed "I love you". I was so tired I could not answer, regretfully! Due to her phone call, I was somewhat relieved thinking I would go back in the morning and everything would be in control and settled down and she would come home shortly! But little did I know this was to be the last time I would ever hear her voice!

The next morning I found her in Intensive Care sedated and asleep. The intensive care nurse said the Doctor would come and see me shortly and I should wait in the coffee room. (I learned later I did not have to leave Intensive care. I should have insisted on staying.) After a while he came and told me that she was totally dependent on the antibiotics she was given. He was nice and I took his statement as positive? (Being an eternal optimist) His demeanor was upbeat with sort of a cautious legalistic ring. I was optimistic and I thought I only had to wait for the antibiotics to do their job. "Sweat it out!"

I called our son Steve who came and spent the night with her. I appreciated it. He was devoted to his mother. Over the next couple of day she did not regain consciousness and was on life support. I began to consider when and if she would recover. I talked to the intensive care nurse, she matter of factly presented the reality of the situation. Bobbie might not recover and if she did she would be brain dead and on life support! For life.

By this time her sister, Addie Jones, and niece Charlie Ann Rotten were visiting. The church minister was there. Reality set in big time. She was probably not going to recover. I began to fear about withdrawing the life support and that she would linger in pain for a long time? So I asked the doctor on his next visit about how long she would linger. He went over and pulled the plug on her life support and everything went to zero instantaneously. Later I was told often patient are held in intensive care just to give the family time to mentally adjust to the reality the patient is gone forever.

Medical Malpractice killed Bobbie. She died from the most common kind of malpractice: outrageous delay in treating her infection. We had been married 50 years. The worst thing is knowing it could have been prevented!

So I got Steve, my son; Addie, Bobbie's sister; Charlie, Addie's daughter, the pastor, and doctor and we all agreed we should pull the plug. Bobbie was gone forever. I sometimes wish I had died. Addie commented: "It seemed everybody got sick on weekend and the doctor was always out of town". The nurses and hospital are all responsible for not getting help.

To this day I have never been able to reconcile all my feeling. My mind is muddled. It goes in a circle. I feel I could have saved her if 0nly I had taken her immediately to the hospital the night before and I should have taking

"At Their Mercy"

control at the hospital. Unnaturally, if only I had not been so child like in my trusting, she could be alive today! This was my frame of mind! I will never forget it! We should always demand that personnel get a doctor.

Looking back, I do not know exactly when the hospital pick up on the fact that Bobbie had a fatal infection. Obviously it was not in time to save her life. My guess is it was late on Saturday July 17th or early on Sunday July 18th. At no time was I ever told anything about an infection risk. I never saw any doctor observing her?

The next thing I remember was talking to Margie Jefferson, a former nurse and fellow political activist who encourage me to file a lawsuit. I want to give Margie credit for being the first to step out. She put the cause of her death to the drug "Methotrexate". "It's bad stuff". One its side effect is it lowers resistance to infections. Another is it causes vomiting. Bobbie was taking Methotrexate from her arthritis Doctor. The drug manufactures advises patients to "Seek medical attention right away if any of these SEVERE side effects occur when using Methotrexate:" The term side effects has always annoyed me. There is no such thing as "side effects". There are only effects. Some are fatal. Side effects are negative symptoms that are not desired.

I also remember Warlick Carr, an attorney friends of Bobbie's, dropping by the house to pay his respects. He encouraged me to sue. She just died too quickly. How could she be well one day and dead the next. It took my breath away.

Junior Bodine

Sudden and unexpected deaths create hardships, long needless pain, which are the worst when you are alone at home. On my lowest day I was sitting at my desk staring at a blood pressure gage thinking I would surely die. I wondered what the blood pressure was for a dying man, so I took it. Unbelievably it was perfect? 120/80. This raised my spirits and spurred my curiosity. How could this happen with all these people who should have been looking out after Bobbie interest: the hospital staff, the doctors, and the nurses. I felt betrayed. And It was not rocket science or brain surgery, It was Ned and the First Reader stuff: simply not attending to the patient. That is what is so pathetic about the whole thing. Her death was so unnecessary when we had the solutions in our very hands and didn't use them. It was senseless!

Bobbie life was a Cinderella story with a tragic ending. She was born on the outskirts of Lubbock the daughter of a share cropper. She attended high school in Lubbock where she won secretarial awards and placed second in the state competition. She was the first of two women to become bank vice presidents in Lubbock and was director of advertising. She wrote the words on the Pioneer Statue at American State bank. We put on her tombstone "The Greatest Woman who ever lived!"

Chapter 2

THE TRUTH ABOUT MALPRACTICE

A Reason to Sue—Something Wrong

Do you have a Medical Malpractice Case? Are you a victim of mal practice? Common sense tells you if you do. And if you do, go with your feeling even though you may also feel : helpless, intimated, inadequate, desperate, utterly alone and a trader to the system, as I did. Most who go to a lawyer don't know exactly why. Go with your passion and sixth sense because this and perseverance may be the determining factor in winning your case. Trust yourself, believe! The happy day is when you win!

Legally if you have negligence and damages; you have a medical malpractice suit . . . (Medical malpractice claims typically result from the negligent conduct of a doctor, nurse, hospital, or other medical staff.) Both negligence and damages are required. Negligence is the failure to perform a duty. Damages are injury, death and monetary. Damages must be the result of the negligence

Given that you have required negligence and damages some attorney's may add a third requirement before they will take a case: Can I Win! Is the patient, surviving spouse, children, beneficiaries or dependents a credible witnesses? What is their Demeanor? Would a jury side with them?

The idea—that a case could be decided not on the merits but on good looks and/or a spellbinding presentation—goes against my nature as a philosophical engineer. But like it or not this is the reality. We make emotional judgments every day on how people present themselves.

Finally you also need the dedication of a kamikaze pilot. And as a former IRS lawyer told me "Do not try to anticipate what they will do". And in my own words "Just stick with the truth and go down the center of the road". You just want justice! This will give you confidence and courage.

There is a 96% chance that all of the above will not be necessary because you will not go to court; your case will be settled out of court. The reason I drag all this up and put the reader through the fundamental law is because, in my opinion, you need to know the fundamental law on which the case is based. There are good reasons for settling out of court: the uncertainty of a jury trial, the $12,000 cost a day to operate a court house plus an overcrowded court docket.

The Reason People Don't Sue

The reason most people don't sue (filed a Medical Malpractice suit) is they can't win. This is best put by a doctor who did sue—a rarity indeed! A unique perspective!

"At Their Mercy"

"I think the malpractice system has run amok" The system is just so rampant with problems. But if you are damaged you are damaged. If we screw up I think we should eat it. The system is a contradiction. Few of the people who deserve compensation actually get any. It is unusual to get compensated. Even so, it involved seven year struggle before all the appeals and challenges were dismissed. At the same time, too many undeserving patients sue Imposing enormous expense and misery. The system, as I see it is fundamentally perverse."

This is our situation in medicine, and litigation has proven to be singularly unsatisfactory solution. It is expensive drawn out, and painfully adversarial. It helps very few people. Ninety-eight percent of American families that are hurt by medical errors don't sue. They are unable to find lawyers who think they would make good plaintiffs, or they are simply too intimidated. Of those that do sue—about fifty-five thousand a year—most will lose. In the end, fewer than one in a hundred deserving families receive any money The rest get nothing: no help, not even an apology. And only the worst is brought out in all of us."

The following is a statement of an outstanding doctor aptly defending doctors. He never filed a Medical Malpractice suit.

"The paradox at the heart of medical care is that it works so well, and yet never well enough. It routinely gives people years of health they otherwise wouldn't have had. Death rates from heart disease have dropped by two thirds, since 1950. Stroke risk has dropped 80%. Cancer survival rates is now 70%. These advances require drugs, machines and operations and most of all decision that can as easily damage people as save them. It is precisely because of the enormous success that people are bound to wonder what went wrong when we fail."

The above is true. We have indeed grown accustom and trusting to what would be described as miracles in prior ages. They are routine and when we have a disaster it is dramatic and unexpected.

But when you put trust, infection and a lack of transparency all together you have a tragedy waiting to happen. These ingredients are just what it takes for tragedy. With trust you do not question, with infection you do not see or hear, and with a lack of transparency you are unaware.

It is instructive to know what the average doctor thinks. He fears, and is infuriated by malpractice suit. They don't want to be sued. (Who does) They say the law is not logical and it is not. According to Judge Andrew P. Napolitano the law is not logical, it is political not just for doctors but for everyone.

Jury trails are vital for justice because they can express the sentiment of the people. Juries can make a statement with the size of their award that expresses moral outrage. Thomas Jefferson was asked why he put the people—a jury—as the final adjudicators. His answer was "Who else would you trust"

The Reason I Sued

I sued because of my wife's post-surgical infection death stemmed from a negligent procedure. The encouragement of a prominent attorney who had been on the hospital board and a former nurse gave me the backbone I needed.

With these endorsements it looks like anyone would have confidently jumped on the case in a New York minute and gone to the pay window for an award or would have been contacted by the hospital! But it did not work that way. There was not a sound. First I had the most difficult task of the whole case: the daunting task of finding a lawyer who would take the case.

At the time, I was sad and lonely and emotionally beat down by shock and emotions. Over shadowing the suit was the fact of just how unfair it was. To be fair the parties must be equal in power and influence. I had neither but I had to take on a powerful and influential medical establishment—a billion dollar business.

Was I naive to think I would win just because I had the facts? Winning was just a matter of staying after it? I had the atomic bomb motivation given by the death of my deceased wife: a moral imperative. Never, ever give up!

The Bigger Picture

Nationally, the discovery of the number of fatalities caused by hospital acquired infection blew me away. There were thousands of preventable death cases each year—similar to Bobbie's—where the patient died from Post-surgical infection stemming from negligent procedure.

Astoundingly the medical community had failed to solve this cascading fatality problem for 164 years, ever since

1847 when it was first discovered that hospitals acquired infections were killing people. It is mind boggling! And you are stunned to learn that the greatest difficulty has been in getting the clinicians to do the one thing that consistently halts the spread of infection: washing their hands; but they continue to wash their hands only a third to a half of the time. It is a senseless phenomenon that spares no one. President Ronald Reagan almost died when he was shot not from the shot but from an infection.

Ten years ago the Institute of Medicine (IOM) declared that as many as 98,000 people die each year needlessly because of preventable medical harm, including health care-acquired infections. Ten years later, they didn't know if we've made any real progress, and efforts to reduce the harm caused by our medical care system were few and fragmented. With little transparency and no public reporting (except where hard fought state laws now require public reporting of hospital infections), scarce data does not paint a picture of real progress. They give the country a failing grade on progress on select recommendations we believe necessary to create a health-care system free of preventable medical harm. In these 10 years 980,000 patients were killed. In the same period there were just 4483 aircraft passengers killed.

Another source says there were 195,000 fatalities due to in hospital medical errors each year that are potentially preventable. This eye-opening figure is an alarming example of how monumental the problem is.

The number of medical fatalities (195,000) has been out there with the admonition that it was not to be given

"At Their Mercy"

to the public. There is a wall of silence. No one speaks out! The Afghanistan war with 355 fatalities makes the headline but hospital medical errors with 195,000 fatalities do not. Nor do the non fatal figures include the 2 million who acquire infection in hospitals. There are 36,915,331 registered hospital admissions each year and 35,149,427 community hospital admission each years. (In dealing with this large numbers sometimes we forget that each one is significant.)

These fatalities undermines the purpose of medical treatment: taking lives, not saving them. The Hippocratic Oath states: "First do no Harm". It may be symbolic that half of the med schools have dropped the Hippocratic Oath! Each new relation completely bowls me over! One hundred ninety five thousands (195,000) is 6 times the number (43,458) killed in automobile accidents each year. Breast cancer takes 42,297, aids 16,516, aircraft 2,087 and the war in Afghanistan 355 U.S. soldiers

Warning: First I don't know exactly what to make of these numbers. They are hard to pin down. The fatality numbers conflict and are underreported by a factor of 4? Their complexity defies a resolution. I have chosen to use 195,000 as the number of fatalities per year.

There is Something Profoundly Wrong with the System!

There is something profoundly wrong with a system that allows 195,000 preventable deaths each year. Who is protecting the patients? The St. Louis Post-Dispatch, published a series of articles titled, "Who Protects the

Patients?" No One! The medical community must be more interested in making money than saving the patient?

Topping this outrageous lost of lives is the outrageous cost. We are spending more the 50% of money spent in the whole world on medical care yet we are only 5% of the world's population! And we are not even in the top 10 when it comes to the longevity of life!

Why do we let 195,000 patients die? Why are we so out of whack? The question is why?

Is there an successful example we can look to where a similar situation has been rectified? The fatalities in a airplane crash is out there for everyone to see.

Flying Fatalities

For 6 year I taught flying and customarily read the accident reports on the investigation of the flying accidents. The way we prevented many deaths is by having strict enforceable rules on how planes must be built, tested, maintained and flown ; and by doing exhaustive studies on every accident? What caused the accident? Was it pilot error? Structural failure or weather? We placed the blame and corrected the problem.

The studies could be lengthy, tedious and time consuming. They could take 6 months or longer and sometimes amounting to trying to find a needle in a haystack. And the penalty can be severe. In one study the pilot and copilot were given 10 year prison sentences for

"At Their Mercy"

the fatalities caused by running out of gas and ditching the airplane.

Why are doctors not held as accountable as airplane pilots? In the worst year for flying accidents there were 1179 aircraft fatalities while hospital fatalities was 195,000 preventable fatalities. One hundred sixty five (165) times the number of aircraft fatalities. In the year 2000 there were 1.6 billion aircraft passengers.

Of course flying an airplane and treating a patient are two different things, but there is a point here.

Lobbying Congress

Unfortunately doctors groups do not place the blame and corrected the infection problem. Instead they hire soulless lobbyist in cahoots with insurances companies to limit their liability.

The Lobbyist for the medical industry told a compelling story about skyrocketing jury awards in malpractice cases forcing insurance rates to rise by 100 percent driving hospitals bankrupt and causing doctors to flee the medical profession. They claimed the solution was to legislate a $250,000 cap on malpractice cases. The American Medical Association of doctors supported this cap.

This story is flat-out-false. Insurance rates are the only thing that soared.

Malpractice suits are one of the few ways in which the medical system can provided an incentive not to take short cuts that hurt the quality of care. Furthermore, the people who will be hurt by a cap of $250,000 are not those who have filed frivolous lawsuits. By definition, they are the people who have proved that they are victims of malpractice, and who has been so badly harmed that a jury has determined they should be significantly compensated.

Due to industry wide cost-cutting, doctors today are being forced to spend less and less time with each patient, and hospital are providing care with fewer and fewer nurses. Standards of care have been compromised, at least to a degree. So if there has been a rise in malpractice payout, changes in the medical delivery system may be part of the explanation.

By capping malpractice settlement, legislatures and congress have turned the most serious victims of our medical system into victims yet again. They have, in effect, made a malpractice case prohibitive. They have disenfranchised the weak and poor. Even winning a lawsuit is a miserable experience.

Lawsuits are not limiting access to health care. The U.S. General Accounting Office found, after an extensive investigation, that doctors groups have been misled, fabricated evidence, or at the very least, wildly overstated their case about how malpractice insurance problems have limited access to health care.

The American Medical Association, a nation organization based in Chicago that represents doctors, and the Physician Insurers Association of America, a coalition of malpractice insurers based in Maryland lobbied for a anti patient nationwide $250,000 cap.

The story of Medical malpractice suits is one of loss wisdom. The fundamental tenet of economics is people respond to incentives. It is Economics 1. Doctors are not punished for failures or rewarded for successes. The failure to understand the role played by incentives is a breakdown of the entire Health Care system to save the lives of patients with preventable fatalities. Not understanding incentive doesn't just apply to doctors and their organization. It applies equally to President Obama and his team and is wrong.

The Health Care business has not solved the medical malpractice problem. Worst yet it is not capable of solving the medical malpractice problem because its culture is so deeply embed. It starts in Med School.

To the casual observer who has no involvement everything may seem OK, but of course this is a myth.

Malpractice Law Suits

The Truth is the doctors and medical system have abandoned the patient and gone the greedy route by pitching in with the soulless lobbyist on capping malpractice awards. Now over half the states have a cap. The claim was that frivolous law and excessive patient awards had driven up insurance premiums. Guess what? The claim was bogus! The cap has had negligible effect on premium

The position of the doctors and the medical system is untenable! They have dumped on the patient. To put a nice face on it I can simply say they do not understand economics and the role incentives play. They route they have taken lowers the cost of killing. What kind of incentive is that?

There is no way you can put a price on the lost of a human. To put a price on one is the height of absurdly. A cap of $250,000 is a disgrace and exhibits the greed and avaricious that abound with these corporations. Losing a 50 year wife provided me the atomic bomb of motivation I needed or I never would have pursued the suit. And to say one size fits all is the height of a lack of common sense. It equates a stumped toe with a fatality.

A $250,000 cap probably amounts to a settlement of $150,000, an attorneys fee of $60,000 and expenses of $20,000 including doctor statement leaving $70,000, a pathetic amount for your wife's life. Beyond the human tragedy, there is the financial tragedy suffered. I loss a car, sold my house, moved out of town and got a job. (Not exactly a get rich quick scheme).

This says nothing of the time and misery involved.

The Reason no one sues.

Paul H. Keckley, director of Deloitte's Center for Health Solution says "The amazing thing is that more patients don't sue." The reason no one sues is they can't win.

"At Their Mercy"

Injured patients rarely file lawsuit . . . And win or lose it is a miserable experience.

The Institute of Medicine, an independent adviser to the government, estimates that as many as 100,000 Americans die yearly from medical mistakes. But only about 4% of injured patients or their families sue, according to a Harvard study. And only 1 in 5 lawsuits awards the patient

Only 4% of the medical malpractice cases filed in North Carolina courts went to verdict (the remaining 96% were settled, dismissed, or resolved in another way). Of those cases that went to verdict, 22.3% were won by the plaintiff. Of those cases won by the plaintiff, the median jury award was $320,000.

Patient

The St. Louis Post-Dispatch published a series last year titled, "Who Protects the Patients? The answer is, of course, no one. Remember no one protecting us citizen.

Apparently, the health care community is more interested in profit than they are in patients. One greedy Health Care executive got a $1 billion benefits packages. One greedy pharmaceutical executive built a $14 million house.

Transparency

There is no transparency. There is no reporting of hospital acquired infections . . . There is no spot light on their activities. There is no public vital information. Dr Phil

Junior Bodine

said in order to solve a problem must admit you have it. Bobbie Knight, the famed basketball coach said doctors should put up a sign, saying 4 cured, 3 died, and 2 hanging in there.

Our only available way to make the medical communities accountable is to be able to sue for unlimited damages.

Chapter 3

PREVENTABLE INFECTION FATALITIES

To go to hospital is a game of Russian Roulette. Granted The odds are in your favor; but you don't know which way the odds are stacked: for you or against you. The first time may be the last time or the last time may be the first time. My brother was given an 80% chance to survive an operation. He died.

Each year there are 195,000 preventable fatalities. Healthgrades a private Denver based company that rates hospitals for health plans and insurers has recently released the results of a survey from all 50 states that revealed that medical errors are responsible for the death of 195,000 people a year in American Hospitals; more than double the estimates provided in earlier studies. These findings make medical mistakes the THIRD LEADING CAUSE OF DEATH in this country behind heart disease and cancer. There is little evidence that patient safety has improved in the last five years according to Dr Samantha Collier vice president of medical affairs at Healthgrades which publishes ranking of hospitals and doctors. Dr Collier has stated that the "equivalent of 390 jumbo jets full of people are dying each year due to likely preventable in-hospital medical errors make this one of the leading killers in the United States"

In accumulating the statistics for this study, HealthGrades utilized a definition of medical errors that includes cases in which hospital staff failed to responds quickly to signs of infection or other dangerous problems, which is an expansion of the definition used in previous studies such as that of JAMA, the Journal of the American Medical Association or that of the Institute of Medicine.

A 1999 study by the institute of Medicine which advises the federal government on heath care issues, used a more limited definition restricting hospital related deaths to overdoses and post surgical infections. That study counted 98,000 deaths in 1999. The HeathGrades figure of 195,000 deaths annually from 2000 to 2002 leads to the conclusion that Americans paid an extra $19 billion in medical care costs for the victims of mistakes.

Patients safety analysts say that HealthGrades' report confirms their belief that the institute of Medicine's death estimate was too low. One of the coauthors of the institute study Dr. Lucan Leape of the Harvard School of Public Heath, has long said his estimate was based on a conservative definition of mistakes that underestimated the real toll.

"At Their Mercy"

Numerous studies support the conclusion that medical errors are widespread harming up to one in 25 patients who are admitted to the hospital.

Dr. Kenneth W. "Kizer of the National Quality Forum, a Washington-based organization that studies health care quality measurement has stated that "this should give you pause when you go to the hospital" He believes that HealthGrades numbers would be even larger if researchers factored in errors of other outpatient settings, such as nursing homes and private doctors' offices.

My discovery of the of the 195,000 fatalities figure came unexpectedly, intensely and distressingly: Thousands of preventable deaths occurring each years!

The outrage was further reinforced when I found that only 1/3 to 1/2 of clinicians went to the trouble to wash their hands; the only thing that consistently halted the spread of deadly infections. Further the medical community had failed to solve the problem caused by hospital acquired infection for 164 years, ever since 1847 when it was first discovered that hospitals were killing people by infection. It is a senseless phenomenon that spares no one. (This seems like a strange outcome for modern day medicine?) President Ronald Reagan almost died when he was shot not from the shot but from an infection. I feel sure his treatment was not delayed. (But what about the 10 of thousands of germs and microbes amounting to pounds that live on our body that are reshaping our view of how people stay healthy?)

My experience on How to prevent a fatality due to infection

10 Tips on saving Lives due to Infections

How do you prevent a fatality due to infection. The answer in a word is "Delay" (Delayed treatment or misdiagnosis are the most common mistakes.) It is not rocket science or brain surgery as it were; it is Ned and the first reader stuff. That is what is so pathetic about the whole thing and so unnecessary when we have the solutions in our very hands but don't use them? It is a Stupid mistake!

- **Tip #1**—Go to the hospital quickly at the first sign of illness! Do not delay. Remember if patient does not exhibit one of the classic symptoms in the Emergency Room then the treatment is normally delayed. On spot examinations can show little. Go with your feeling and instincts. You know how you feel and your history. (Remember you are the only full time witness for your entire life.)
- **Tip #2**—Do not delay in talking to doctors. Don't pussy foot around. Tell them your feeling and instincts. Ask questions. They are required to give you an answer. Don't let them nice you to death.
- **Tip #3**—Did not allow them to let you sit around emergency room all day. My mistake! Insist on immediate treatment. Do not assume they know what they are doing and have put your history, doctors and medication all together—verify. Or as President Reagan said "trust but verify".
- **Tip #4**—Remember they are dealing with thousands of patients (shootings, car wreck, etc.) that are more dramatic visible injures and Infection is unseen

and unheard but just as deadly. You are dealing with just you and you have only you—the most significant patient in the world just you!

Tip #5—Make list of medications and doctors carry it in your pocket. Half people die from prescription drugs; more than die from illegal drugs. There is no one in the world who can tell you exactly how they will all medication interact or react. That is the state of the medical culture.

Tip #6—Tell doctors if you have drug allergies

Tip #7—When given a drug. Ask what it is and what it is for.

Tip #8—Speak up if you sense something is wrong. This may be a little intimidating but your busy doctor of nurse may have overlooked something and your concern may be the only warning they get.

Tip #9—Inquire about taking antibiotics

Tip #10—**Take notes**. Stay with patient night and day and keep written notes on everything: date and time of medication and what for; date and time of doctor and nurse visits everything! Take the lead in looking after the operation, the medications and the body itself. They may ask you to leave the room but they can't make you. Ask doctors and nurses what is going on. You can't assume. Can't take word. Have someone there all the time. Can't be nice. Don't leave the room. The public does not know a damn thing that goes on in hospitals. It is not the same as when I grew up.

If you do not keep notes and there is a dispute or a lawsuit, the hospital has all the medical records and you have nothing but your word and and they won't take your word.

Chapter 4

LAWYERS

Warlick Carr, the attorney, gave me the confidence to win this lawsuit. He was not just any lawyer he was a world class lawyer in spades. He was twice voted the most ethical lawyer in the state of Texas. His brother Waggoner was the Attorney General of the State of Texas when President John F. Kennedy was assassinated in Dallas. He was Bobbie's banking friend and I was his tennis friend. He had an office high in the largest office building in town.

Mot all lawyers are not held in such high esteem because they work for the government, the banks, the rich and the powerful pitted against the common man. And often they win not by upholding the law but by circumventing it. The champion of the little guy is the lawyer in the small store front office.

Old timers said when the lawyers and bankers take over a town it is time to move on . . .

"At Their Mercy"

A survey showed that the general public hates lawyers. The Lawyers respond that it is because of their image as portrayed on TV. But Jerry Spence voted the number one lawyer at the time, said: "No! it was because of direct personal contact". Jerry Spence spent his lifetime representing the poor, the injured, the forgotten and the damned against what he calls "The new slave master", a combine of mammoth corporations and gargantuan government. He never lost a criminal case.

Hating lawyers is not a recent thing. Shakespeare, who died on April 23, 1616, in his quote from "King Henry V" said: "The first thing we do, let's kill all the lawyers." No doubt, there are some slime ball lawyers. A good example is some lawyer who won a big class action suit and turned right around and stole $200 million from their clients, the injured who were left destitute. The attorneys went to jail. Aren't lawyer responsible for the fine print disclaimers you see everywhere costing the country an estimated $250 billion?

Two third of the world lawyers live in this country. They dominate the legislature and are one of the largest political contributors. It cost $100,000 to go to Georgetown law school and a graduate can expect to make $160,000.

I have often been to Texas Tech Law Library. It is a showplace. There is a spacious parking lot. The building is a very impressive, brick structure with narrow windows (like a mosque) and brick floors. The recreation room has an 18 foot high ceiling. An elaborate large section of the building was added by an alumina who won a big settlement.

The building is perfect for studying. It is quiet and sparsely populated. The student seems dedicated, well dressed and friendly. Most speak. Every book is in its place on the shelve. The atmosphere resembles a quiet palace.

In my research there, I was shocked to find the laws are fair beyond my wildest dream. Unbeknown to me a government agency select the laws supporting its position and present them as the gospel to an unknowing public. Even with the laws precisely fitting the citizens position he can not get justice. He is given the run around and it is made too hard for the average citizen who can't get a lawyer. The poor people can not afford a lawyer . . . I think it is lamentable that the poor receive no justice. Government agencies make it all but impossible to handle your own claim. Rarely does a common man get justice. Then it takes the courage of a gorilla and the determination of a Kamikaze pilot. A criminal charged with murder put everything in perspective when he said of our legal system "You are innocent until proved broke".

And lawyers who can get millions for multi million corporations make million. Consequently they are always looking for individuals with real power and money: the important and rich client! However without the support of a lawyer and a nurse I would never have filed a claim.

Warlick Carr was an attorney who gave lawyers a good name. He dropped by and gave me the necessary legal encouragement. My retired nurse friend came by and give me the necessary medical encouragement. The two of them made my case legitimate. I was on the map.! Without them, I would have never filed this suit. Unfortunately,

Warlick was not a medical malpractice attorney. So, sadly I had to look elsewhere; and, that opened a whole new can of worms

Since a lawyer is at once your savior and your adversary it bears looking at the legal profession and getting the lay of the legal landscape. I following a line of investigating cases that included the Law Library, TV, newspaper, magazines, the public library and any thing that got my eye or ear anywhere I happen to be.

Specifically in malpractice suits it is not a case of finding a good attorney; it is a case of finding any attorney who will take the case. The lawyer in a malpractice suit bears all expenses and only get paid if he wins (no recovery, no fee) so he takes only the cases he thinks he can win. That does meant he will win. After all the law is political not logical as many people think. Getting a lawyer validates the legitimacy of your suit in your mind. It gives you confidence. Normally one lawyer will turned down 8 malpractice cases before taking one. Just by coincident I was turned down 8 times before I eventually found a lawyer who would take my case. I had a friend who sued a major oil company and could not get an attorney to take his case. Finally he wound up with a drunk and was successful. So my case as well as his case was not one of being egged on by a greedy lawyer. Far from it.

Warlick first took me to a meeting with a fellow lawyer at his very large meeting room The room was full of lawyers and secretaries taking notes. The meeting made a lot sense to them but it was a total disaster for me. I was emotionally overwhelmed and unhinged. It was the first time I had confronted my whole situation in its entirety. The whole world comes crashing down on me. I was center stage. I was still in mourning! This lawyer wanted a large retainer. I could not afford one! I wanted a lawyer with no retainer which I learned is standard in medical malpractice suits. I learned that generally attorneys take medical malpractice suits on a contingency basis because the victim can ill afford to pay an attorney. And above all if the attorney don't think enough of your case to take it on contingency then you don't want him anyway.

After that I went alone to a young lawyer office. He was the current leading young lawyer in town. He had receive a multi-million dollar settlement and had a fallacious two story office building and even though they were the most accommodating they did not take the case and as a matter of fact I found that the rule that local lawyers do not sue local banks and hospital? But that is a whole other story. Nonetheless, they made me feel good because they just extruded an air of polite confidence in turning me down.

Then the next lawyer took my case. He was out of town and the legal aide I was dealing with had been a nurse. It was no fun? They seemed somewhat taken with themselves in an academic way. Although we had several conversations and quite a lot of correspondence he later turned down my case? I read and reread his turn down letter. Naturally I was disappointed but in another way I felt relieved. We never connected! At the time It was a big blow! I had gotten only one lawyer and he quit! But, it turned out for the best: I got another better Lawyer with which I connected.

"At Their Mercy"

The following lawyers I approached are a blur. One actually ask me for a letter saying I did not hire him evidently for fear of losing hospital work? I was puzzled for what it implied: The hospital had a dead grip on lawyers. As a courtesy, I gave him a letter.

Then I remember talking to a attractive sounding lady lawyer in Dallas who I tried extra hard to get to take the case because we hit it off. I press her : "Why won't you take the case?" She said I do not take medical malpractice cases anymore because "Every time I take a medical mal practice suit I lose."

Finally I got a Dallas attorney; suggested to me by a lawyer at our church. It turned out he had gone to Texas Tech and played on the tennis team. His wife was a doctor. I hit it off perfectly with his girl there in the office who was knowledgeable about the law and was compassionate. We could not have dovetailed more perfectly. Unfortunately she left before the case was over; thankfully the case was all set by then. I continued to do research and keep my lawyer covered up with notes.

Once equipped with a lawyer I was ready for the games to begin. A malpractice suit is unfair; its outrageous. The big, highly proclaimed legal picture is that there is "equal justice for all". This is a lie: a publically held false impression. There can be no equal justice unless both parties have equal wealth and influence. Doctors and Hospitals have plenty of money and they use it to influence laws capping their liabilities and hiring top notch lawyers. Texas, which enacted some of the most extensive malpractice reforms in the nation in 2003. Governor Bush pushed through a law limiting settlement to $250,000 that It is way too low. Malpractice suit are a welfare for doctors due to number of doctors statement required. So it would be me (with no wealth or influence) vs the billion dollar hospital and insurance company. Once at a political event I found myself standing next to an Appeals Court Judge... I asked him if a common man could get justice?. His answer was not comforting: "rarely". I appreciated his candor. Meanwhile it burned me that a hospital lawyer drove around in a black $100,000 car.

After getting a lawyer the pressure seemed to be off. My position was validated. The lawyer would carry the ball. I continued to research but at a leisurely pace. We communicated by phone, email and letters. Shortly my case came out in the paper. And my attorney John visited in our house once. Our next face to face visit was the hearing: a meeting with the other side including the doctor and some attorneys and a judge paid for by me. My attorney John told me if he kicked me under the table to stop that line of the conversation. The other side asked me questions which I do not remember except one: "was my wife throwing up"? I said: "No" three time. I got the strangest feeling. When I got home, with my notes to refresh my memory, I found my wife was certainly "throwing up". In fact that was the deciding reason I took her to the hospital. I had completely blocked it from my mind. At first I had thought I had blown the case until I stopped and thought it was certainly the type of thing I would block from my mind, which I evidently did, because it was so painful. The only other thing of note that came up was a thank you note I had written to the head nurse who visited intensive care to see Bobbie.

Again I felt like I had sort of hurt myself but it raised the question of what was her motive for visiting intensive care. I felt confident. I had told the truth but I was not completely at ease. Further I heard that she and the nurse going off duty got into an argument in the stair well about whether Bobbie should be taken to intensive care. I told my attorney John who gave no response?

John continued talking to the other side. He asked me if I wanted for the checks sent to him. I said: "yes!" That was a mistake. At the time, I was thinking: I can't go through all this again and get another lawyer. I had unreasoned fears it would jeopardy the suit. John gave double entry bookkeeping a whole new meaning.

There is a $250,000 cap in Texas, on medical malpractice law suit. It is too low. Just attorney fees are 40% for lst $125,000 and 33.3% for next $125,000. Expenses are $50,000. This is without the damages and lost due to the patient death.

I liked my attorney John.

My last contact with him was in a bitter sweet telephone conversion. I felt cut off and alienated! I had my heart in my hand. In a strange way I hated to see it end because it had gone on for so long. He closed by saying "In life our trails cross and we move on". All of this had been such a emotional roller coaster ride. I can't be certain but it felt like he said "don't call me I will call you!"

Chapter 5

DOCTORS

Sir Anthony Carlisle England (1768-1840) English Surgeon.

"Medicine is an art founded on conjecture
and improved by murder"—

Some say the medical profession is the oldest profession in the world? The first thing God did with humans was to performed an operation: he took out Adams rib and made Eve. The medical profession may or may not be the oldest profession in the world but it is one of the most popular all over the world. A twenty first century phenomena.— hyper popular. It is harder to get into medical school than it is the engineering school. Doctors go to school for 11 years. (4 years of college, 4 years of medical school and 3 years of residency.)

Doctor are highly respected and revered. I have always respected and even reveled doctors with good reason: I owe my life to them. They saved both my wife's and my lives. My wife Bobbie had 50 years of successful medical experience with 13 successful major operations including

"At Their Mercy"

3 for cancer. Some were life saving. I remember one of these operations distinctly. It was a weekend emergency room trip where she was operated on for a twisted intestine. In the patient room every time I looked up the doctor was examining her surgery for infection! I took the medical profession for granted and had a childlike trust for doctors. They are the heart and soul of our medical system. They are it's center, it's public face. They have status and position in the community.

Doctors are special people who sacrifice family life. My personal 70 years of medical experience with doctors has gone very well. I had 4 operations: the reduction of enlarged prostate, the repair of a rupture, the removal of section of my the colon and the installation of heart stints.

A long time ago a local Dermatologist kept treating my penis rash which kept getting worst. Alarmed, I changed Dermatologist only to suffer the same fate! Finally I went to the Mayo Clinic in Minneapolis, as a walk on for my skin condition. They discovered I was allergic to the binder in my medication. I clearly remember the handsome young doctor was silent as we sat in his office looking out the window for what seemed like an eternity. It was the first time I felt like I had my say with a doctor and the irony of it all was I actually said very little

I had a friend who reported to the Mayo Clinic in Florida for a heart operation only to be told he did not need it! He was so elated and thankful that he talked to the doctor for 30 minutes, finally he said: "I had better get out of here so you can make some money operating." The doctor said

"I make the same amount of money talking to you as I do for operating!"

These two Mayo Clinic stories illustrate the value of having a doctors on a salary taking the time to satisfy the patient as opposed to having a doctor getting paid by the test and procedures where sometimes you can't even get the time of day

When Doctors are compensated for each test and procedure. they spent less time with the patient and more time doing unnecessary tests and procedures that generate more revenue.

There are 853,187 physician in the U.S.A. They are perceived as rich for good reason they are the highest paid in the world. Their medium pay is $210,000. Their pay ranges from $150,000 to $350,000. This (853,187 x 210,000) amounts to a total of $179,169,270,000 billion a year. The decision of the Medicare Payments Advisory Commission (MPAC) is that Specialists should face a 50% pay cut and GPs a 30% cut.

When the general public is asked for the cause of the high cost of our medical system they point to the hospitals and doctors. The doctors do not deserve a pass for they have taken off their halo to put their interest above that of the patient. The unvarnished truth is that doctors, through the American Medical Association, have donated million to lobbyist for stupid incentives that avoid paying 80% of harm inflicted on patients and families. (Of course the real problem is medical malpractice not medical malpractice lawsuits.) But above and beyond this there is something which is just not right morally or legally about our health care system.

A young physician puts the blame on the patient: Cultural Crisis. "During my shift in the Emergency Room I had a patient with a shiny gold tooth, whose body was adorned with costly tattoos, and who wore expensive shoes. She chatted on a new expensive cell phone. Her payer status was 'Medicaid'. She smoked a pack of cigarettes and drank beer everyday. Our "health care crisis" is not the result of a shortage of quality hospitals, doctors or nurses. It is a culture crisis based on the irresponsible credo that "I can do whatever I want to because someone else will take care of me". Once you fix this 'culture crisis' you'll be amazed at how quickly our nation's health care difficulties disappear?"

Chapter 6

NURSING

Florence Nightingale (1820-1910)

Florence Nightingale laid the foundation for modern day professional nursing with founding of her nursing school in London in 1860. But her most famous contribution came during the Crimean War in Istanbul which became her central focus when reports began to filter back to Britain about the horrific conditions for the wounded. She and her nurses found wounded soldiers being badly cared for by overworked medical staff in the face of official indifference. Medicines were in short supply, hygiene was being neglected, and mass infections were common, many of them fatal. There was no equipment to process food for the patients.

During her first winter at Scutari, 4,077 soldiers died there. Ten times more soldiers died from illnesses such as typhus, typhoid, cholera and dysentery than from battle wounds. Conditions at the temporary barracks hospital were fatal to the patients because of overcrowding and the hospital's defective sewers and lack of ventilation.

"At Their Mercy"

At the beginning of the 20th century, it was asserted that Nightingale reduced the death rate from 42% to 2% either by making improvements in hygiene herself.

In her own words she said the honor of being a nurse does not lie in putting on Nursing like your uniform. The Honor lies in loving perfection, consistency, and in working hard for it.

Today, we need a Florence Nightingale, who would stand up for badly treated patients and an overworked nursing staff so that screaming patients are not ignored and deaths prevented.

150 billion civil award—servant of the people "moral outrage"—never see the money—civil justice system Loyola Marymount school of law Las Angeles—make statement—biggest civil verdict—want message to be heard, it needs to be significant; this is how people hear about these things—truth put matter to rest—refuse to take issue—make a stink—make a statement

CHAPTER 7

NUMBERS

The Big Figures—It is impossible to know exact numbers because no independent authority examines the records of hospitals, doctors and drug companies.

U.S. Economy—

U.S. Economy	$14.7 Trillion
Health Care	$2.6 Trillion

Who Protects Patient—Medical Malpractice Lawsuit
Each year there are 195,000 fatalities due to in hospital medical errors that are potentially preventable. The following are representative fatality figures.

Hospital Fatalities	195,000
Aircraft Fatalities (Highest)	3,214
Motor Vehicle	43,458
Breast Cance	42,297
Aids	16,516

"At Their Mercy"

Lobby Spending—

Total Lobbying spending 1998-2011 $31.98 billion
Total Health Sector $4.62 billion
Pharmaceutical $2.20 billion

Drugs—

Non Toxic Drugs	17,000 Drugs
Toxic Drugs	6,000 Drugs
Illegal Drugs	$48.4 billion

Salaries—

    Salaries   Number

Physician

$216,000 medium	853,187
($186,004) 2008	(661,400) 2008

Lawyers

$110,950	759,200

Pharmacist—$104,260   269,900

*Salaries shown are a median. Specialties can be sever times higher

Junior Bodine

Largest Market for illegal drugs—At the same time that we are the most medicated country in the world with prescription drugs, we are also the single largest marketplace for illegal drugs. The U.S. Department of Justice estimates that wholesale earnings from illicit drug sales range from $13.6 billion to $48.4 billion annually.

We are over medicated—The problem of overmedication is tragic. About half our youth have taken drugs. Most don't realize it is killing us. Many have come to rely on pills which are constructed by man in a laboratory. Pills that do not balance our body, mind, and spirit. Often these toxic pills pollute our bodies and disturbs our vitality and weakens our immune system and become fatal. They are poisoning us? There is too much pill popping. Using IV drugs take 15 year off your life. L. Pitts of Miami Herald, wrote 1.3 % of the population are **drug addicts** which is the same as 1924. (One point three (1.3 %) percent of our current population is 4,290,000 (.013 x 330,000,000 = 4,290,000)

More die from prescription drug—More people die from legal (prescription) drug than die from illegal drugs. Posted on the corridor wall of the recovery room at UMC was a notice saying over half of all deaths are caused by medications.

One out of 20 people become drug abusers. Eighty one (81)% percent of a college football team failed the drug test. This does not prove they are addicts. It simply means they had taken a drug at the time.

Edition

Prominent Figures dies—When Prominent entertainment figure die from drug overdoses it opens the curtain a little. Michael Jackson was killed by the overdose of the anesthetic *propofol*, in June 2009. Drugs killed the King of Rock and Roll Elvis Presley. Whitney Houston died from a combination of prescription drugs and illegal drugs mixed with alcohol?

Scary state of pharmacy—The real story is that we are in the stone age of prescription drugs, the scary state of pharmacy There are 17,000 drugs and 6,600 toxic drugs and nobody can knows exactly how they all interact . . . There has been no medicine that is not sensitive to someone. A local drug store carries 75-100 medications. Some carry 200 drug. There is a book "The Pill Book" that sit on the counter of my druggist (Amigo Pharmacy) that purports to be a complete Illustrated guide on drug interactions? It sells for $10. I bought a book "Prescription Drug for people over 50" at a garage sale for 50 cents. In it's 576 pages it list about 200 drugs with the admonition to: talk to your doctor or pharmacist whenever you have a question. The facts are that too often we can not get the time of day from doctors and pharmacist.

We should always know what pills we're taking—and what side effects they might cause. And we should always read the label and follow directions before taking any medication. But! bull corn! There is no human being on the face of the earth who can read that too small print of pages and pages of that stuff. It is known as a disclaimer:

Layer and layers of written fine print stuff to baffle and confuse readers and deny any liability. It is estimated that this lawyer written fine print of all kinds cost us citizen $500 billion dollars a year. You know what the lawyer say when asked about this "too small to read print?" They say "we don't get any complaint from our clients"?

Pharmaceuticals are a slippery slope (Indeed the whole Medical field is) that range from miracles cures to devastating failures. Often taking drugs is a crap shoot. Reading about drugs is a turn off. The labels are incomprehensible. Go with your instinct: what gives you peace of mind . . . Hopefully the labels will be made readable.

Drugs worsen Schizonphrena—Some recreational and prescription drugs appear to cause or worsen symptoms of schizophrenia. They manifests themselves as <u>auditory hallucinations</u>, <u>paranoid</u> or bizarre <u>delusions</u>, or <u>disorganized speech and thinking</u>, and it is accompanied by significant social or occupational dysfunction.

Real War is Here—Our real war is here at home taking care of ourselves. It is not in some far away place on the other side of the world like Afghanistan where they have been fighting for 10,000 years. It is here in our own country. We must boldly confront our problems. Congress is not looking out for us. Doctors are looking out for themselves. The pharmaceutical industry certainly looks after themselves in spades. We must take personal responsibility and look after ourselves. It is like the old man said "If you are not for you, then that makes it unanimous."

This is Money Country—This is a money country. It is run by organized money and money elects our politicians. The Pharmacy Industry have spend billions on lobbyist that profit them big time. They are the top industry contributors to lobbyist. They spent $2.2 billion of the total lobby spending of $31.98 billion (1998-2011). Lobbyist lobby congress. Congressmen spend 70 % of their time raising campaign contribution to get reelected. Ninty five percent (95%) do get reelected.

From book **"So Damn much money"** (The triumph of lobbying and the corrosion of American Government) by Robert G. Kaiser.

"So Damn Much Money is an accurate and frank description of how lobbyist and money have come to run Washington. It is very much in the spirit of the great muckraking books at the turn of the twentieth century". Leon Panetta

There is an army of Lobbyists that Puts Drug Company and HMO Profits ahead of Patients and Taxpayers, "Public Citizen Congress Watch", June 2004,

There are 4 times as many lobbyists as there are congressmen. According to the Center for Responsive Politics, in 2005 there were 2,084 health care lobbyists registered with the federal government. With 535 members of Congress, that's about 4 lobbyists per member.

Drug Commercial—TV is killing us with sex, news and drug commercials. Everyday there are 24 hours of advertising food and drugs. Guess what! We wind up with obesity and drug addicts. Everyday millions of people get suckered by dubious claims of miraculous cures by scaremongers. And they don't just fall for the claims once—they get fooled again and again. We are brain washed. There is an epidemic of prescriptions. Some patients spend $1000 a day. There has got to be a limit!—TV CNN 12:10 October 10, 2011. Some people can be suckered into a drug life style by constant not worth watching TV drug commercials. For every 8 minutes of programs there are 3 paralyzing minutes of commercials.

Doctor through their professional organization the American Medical Association spend millions to get legislation that profits them at patients expense . . .

The political clout of the medical profession is overwhelming. In the US, drug companies spend $19 billion a year on promotions. Too much of the public is hooked on pill popping

Political Campaign Contributions—A study by Citizen Action, a consumer group, reports that doctors, hospitals, insurance companies and other providers of medical services made campaign contributions of $ 79 million during the 1993-1994 election cycle. The insurance industry passed out $16 million. The American Medical Association, which objects to cost-control measures, contributed $ 3 million. "The big lie about health reform," Rocky Mountain News, August 20, 1995.

Executive Compensation—Executive compensation for the Pharmaceutical Industry will knock your socks off.

1. Michael B McAllister earned $3.33 million in compensation as CEO of Humana. "Forbes 2006 Executive Pay list," April 20, 2006.
2. John W Rowe earned $22.2 million in compensation as CEO of Aetna. Rowe has since left Aetna. "Forbes 2004 Executive Pay list," April 21, 2005.
3. Bill McGuire has stock options worth $1.6 billion at the end of 2005, as CEO of United Health Group.
4. Robert Simison, "SEC Investigates United Health Over Stock-Options Practices," Bloomberg News"

<u>Fourteen Congressional aides went to work for the Pharmical industry; Billy Tauzin left Congress to become CEO of PhRMA for a $2 million annual salary.</u>

Lawsuit against Johnson & Johnson—A good illustration of the greed in pharmacy is shown by the size of a lawsuit against Johnson & Johnson:

A South Carolina Judge upheld a $327 Million verdict against Health giant Johnson & Johnson for overstating safety and effectiveness of former blockbuster antipsychotic drug, Risperdal. The pill for schizophrenia and bipolar disorder once brought J&J more than $3.4 billion annual sales. J&J has been mired for years in litigation over alleged kickbacks, promotion for unapproved uses. Dozens of pending cases allege illegal marketing practices. Including one in Texas seeking more than $1 billion.

Greed—Some soulless Drug Companies are the very epitome of Greed. They exploit every opportunity. During a drug shortage they resorted to collusion and price gouging—profiting big time. During one drug shortage a drug usually costing $26 was offered for $1200.

A cancer drug was marked up to $650 from $50 in an emergency shortage situation. (as reported on national TV by Brain William 11/17/11 NBC)

Top pharmaceutical drugs—Listed below are the top 4 drugs by Retail Sales

Drug	Manufacturer	Sales	For
1—Nexium—	AstraZeneca Pharmaceuticals	$ 5,276,153,000	Acid Reflux
2—Lipitor—	Pfizer.Inc	$5,272,576,000	Heart
3—Plavix—	Bristol-Myers Squibb Company	$4,675,483,000	Heart
4—Adair Diskus—	GlaxoSmithKline—	$3,655,206,000	Asthma

Doctors are too busy to dig into the statistics of cancer treatments, they assume that what they are taught at school or what is demonstrated in the pages of briefing journals is the best treatment. They cannot afford to suspect that these treatments are only the best for the pharmaceutical companies that influence their 'institutions of higher learning'. Paul Winter, The Cancell Home Page, dedicated to exposing the fraud behind pharmaceutical company controlled medical research institutions and their deliberate withholding of information from the general public on safe cancer treatments.

The Colossal Demand—

So far we have talked about the gigantic size of the supply of drugs and treated everyone as a victim. When the truth of the matter is the "victims" are the demander of drugs . . . There would never be this supply unless there was this demand for drugs for whatever reason.

Chapter 8

CONCLUSION— FINAL II— THIS IS MASTER COPY

My wife death inspired this intensely personal book. . . Despite the fact she was throwing up every 4 minutes and hollering "Somebody Help me"; The hospital delayed her treatment all day and half the night before someone showed up to treat her.

Her unexpected, preventable death was senseless. Stunning! It was not some complicated life saving operation gone wrong that killed her but just simply a "No Show".

Since then I have never let my mind deviate from the one central reality that there is a need for this book: a true life story that could save lives. And I hope my winning fight of the malpractice suit will be an inspiration to others. If it is, Bobbie would not have died in vain.

"At Their Mercy"

When I started writing this book in 2004 I had a simplistic view of our medical system. There were just Doctors, Nurses, Hospitals and a corrupt and dysfunctional Washington . . . This distant capital, which looms over us all, does not live under the same laws we do. . . They pass laws which give them unlimited health care and giant lifetime salaries. (Laws are best passed by people who live under them.) Washington is not listening to "we the people/". They are listening to them the lobbyist. Our elected officials spend 70% of their time raising money to get reelected. Ninety five (95)% get reelected. They want to stay on this gravy train.

1. The first thing I learned, in 8 years of research, is that the root cause of my wife's death was a preventable infection. Although the most effective prevention (washing hands) has been known for over 164 year, from 30 to 50 percent of the time clinicians go from room to room without washing their hands. Amazingly these deaths continue? In fact 195,000 patients die each year from preventable infections. This is a tragic figure! Something is profoundly wrong! Our unquestioning submission corrupts our leaders and demeans our subordinates.

2. The second thing I found was our medical system is corporate tyranny and stupid incentives. We have highly complex private for profit insurance and a jungle like fragmented system. Profit health care is evil. Insurance companies put profit above patients. Our system is a combine between mammoth corporations and gargantuan government. This serves politicians and corporations but people pay the price. We, in this country, spend half ($2.7 trillion) of all the money

spent in the world on health care. (Hospitals, doctors and pharmaceuticals take 61% of our healthcare cost: respectively 31, 20 and 10 percent.) And we are not even in the top ten when it comes to longevity of life (But to be fair there are two side to the longevity of life: the medical care of the patient on one hand and the life style of the patient on the other hand. In Utah, a clean living Mormon state, their longevity of life is 80.08 years. While the state of Nevada has a longevity of life of 77.59 year . . . The life expectancy of Mormons, just as a group, is 84 years. None the less, at the end of the day we still spend $2.7 trillion and are out of the top ten when it come to longevity of life for the whole country.)

3. The third thing I learned is we got corporate gangsters stealing us blind. We give illegal's amnesty and free healthcare. Some great companies are getting slaughtered by Healthcare. We have indefensible high administrative cost. Many individuals go bankrupt and/or die because they can not afford medical bills. Some die because they are uninsured.

4. The fourth thing I leaned is the ugly truth about doctors is they have spent billions of dollars through the American Medical Association lobbying and passing stupid incentive laws that undermine the safety of health care but benefit them. . . One such law drastically caps the amount of the award in malpractice suits. (While the real crisis is medical mistakes not medical lawsuits.) Instead of reducing fatalities this new law encourages them.

The first law of economics 1 is on incentives. This economic law as applied to medical malpractice lawsuits says if you want fewer malpractice suits you make their

"At Their Mercy"

cost higher to doctors. Has anybody ever heard of the word "pain"? Thus doctor are encouraged not to make mistakes injuring patients. Conversely if you lower the cost of lawsuits doctors are not as motivated to avoid mistakes. This causes more deaths.

This cap is patently absurd! But it is symptomatic of our Health Care System. . . The patients are indeed under attack. This brings me back to the theme of this book!

Who protects the patient?

5. The fifth thing I learned is there is no accountability: No one is responsible. Somebody has got to be in charge from start to finish. Patients are treated like a bunch of fire hydrants. Doctors and hospitals abandon the patient. There is a wall of silence
6. The sixth thing I learned is that Emergency Rooms are the backbone of health care. Typically one Emergency Room handles 97 patients in 12 hours. I read an article about a doctor in the "Parade" section of Sunday paper who charged $5 for an office visit, saw 120 patients a day and did not accept private insurance?
7. The seven thing I learned is that I am not a doctor or politician. I am an engineer and I know that I am the world's greatest authority on me and my experience.
8. The eight thing I learned was there are politicians with answers. Former President Bill Clinton said we are letting politics get in the way of a solution. In health care we have done nothing but debate on whether to debate on healthcare. We have done little to move forward. We need to think and weight evidence of what works in real life and debate not on whether to debate but on how

to do it. This sounds like a local initiative involvement to me.
9. The ninth thing I learned was the answer to questions about medical care and pharmaceutical getting so complicated that no one understands. My wife's doctor said: "It is simple. It is just like grandma told us if you go out in the sun put on a bonnet, cover your arms, eat lots of fruits and vegetables fiber and stay away from too much red meat" An 81 year lady said: "Don't take medicine unless you have a screaming pain. Medicine cures this and causes that."
10. The tenth thing I learned was our only hope for fairness and justice in medical care is in the people. The will of people can make difference with **human feelings and common sense :** their deepest human instincts. But unless we share info we will get nowhere. We the people need to center the process of health on the informed individual so he or she can have the knowledge, desire, responsibility and opportunity to live the longest life, with the best health, at the lowest cost.
11. The eleventh thing I learned is our best prescription for health may not be one you—will get from a doctor—economy equality. This according to Stephen Bezruchla, M.D.who taught at the University of Washington's School of Public Health.

In the February 26, 2001 issue of Newsweek he said "It is a disgrace that we are the 25[th]country in longevity given that we are the riches country in the world and spend half of all the money spent in the world on healthcare."

Japan is no 1 in the world when it comes to longevity. They are organized to where their citizen share equally in the economy. During crisis, managers take pay cuts rather than laying off workers.

We in the United States are 25th in the world because of our gap between the rich and the poor. How does this affect our health. For those that are at the top they feel power, domination and coercion. For those that are at bottom they feel resignation, resentment and submission. With economic equality everyone would feel support, friendship, cooperation and sociability.

Ha-Joon Chang, a South Korean, teaches economics at Cambridge University. He is the author of the book **"23 Things They Don't Tell You About Capitalism"**. Thing 14 is "U.S. managers are over-priced and the politics of class envy" The CEO compensation in the U.S. is 300-400 times the salary of the average worker. Some CEO make 500 times the average worker. If that were the case then his CEO would make $20,000,000 and he would make $20,000.

Staying informed is a matter of life and death

www.ingramcontent.com/pod-product-compliance
Lightning Source LLC
Chambersburg PA
CBHW021021180526
45163CB00005B/2057